BEYOND GRADUATION

3 Mission Critical Strategies for Launching a Successful Career

Larry Johanson

BEYOND GRADUATION
Copyright © 2015 by Larry Johanson

All rights reserved. No part of this book may be reproduced or transmitted in any form or by any means without written permission from the author.

ISBN 978-0-9917317-3-2

Published in Canada by Becoming Achievers Seminars

Dedication

For Matthew who vows not to let school get in the way of his education.

Table of Contents

Dedication 3
Preface 7
A Note to You the Graduate 9
My Story 13
Clarify Your Mission and Purpose 19
Cultivate the Achiever's Mindset 43
The Four Strategic Moves 65
Conclusion 105
Courses, Seminars, Workshops 107

Preface

This book is for college and university students who are about to graduate or have already graduated and are wondering what steps to take to launch their career.

My decision to write this book and create this program came after I was invited to give a presentation to a class of college students a few weeks from graduation on the importance of marketing and positioning themselves in the job market. Minutes into the presentation after asking some basic questions to see how ready they were to launch their career I realized that the majority of them were woefully unprepared.

Many of them had already completed a first degree and had taken this college course, presumably to give themselves some more practical and marketable skills, yet they seemed to be at a loss about their next steps.

I came away very troubled because they put me in mind of myself who graduated decades earlier with a Masters degree in Communication Studies without giving any serious thought to what my next steps would be on graduation. The result was that I lost precious momentum, time, energy and money trying out one job and potential career after another and only stumbled into my present career after much trial and error.

My unconditional guarantee to the college and university graduate fortunate enough to find this book and smart enough to implement the strategies and techniques is that they will have a proven blueprint or roadmap that will, at the very least, increase their chances of living the life they want on their terms. Most importantly they will gain a competitive advantage over their peers in the marketplace.

A Note to You the Graduate

Congratulations! You have finally graduated. Walking across the stage bedecked in your mortar board and gown to collect your diploma is a special moment, one to be savored. Your proud parents more than likely shared this moment with you and your graduation pictures will probably be placed in a prominent place in your house, a memento of your achievement and an example for your children to follow. You have arrived at this moment because of a great deal of discipline and hard work and now with a gleam in your eyes and brimming with hope and optimism you prepare to embrace your future. You have followed the advice of parents and teachers; been assured that this was the way to go and now you look forward to being rewarded for your efforts with a great job that pays you the money to afford the lifestyle you have dreamed of.

But there are troubling signs on the horizon. Big bold headlines in the newspaper speak of layoffs, downturn in industries and economies around the world; of jobs shifting and moving offshore to economies where labor is cheap and benefits non-existent. You start sending out résumés but you get no response and you worry that instead of spreading your wings you might have to confine yourself to your parents' basement for the foreseeable future. And all the while the interest on your student loan and credit card debt continues to compound and grow. The optimism and hope you felt on graduating begin to be overshadowed with pessimism and gloom.

To add insult to injury you realize that you and your peers, the millennials, born between 1982 and 2004 have been dubbed with the dubious title, "Generation Screwed". You learn that you are the most highly educated and indebted generation going into the job market but face the prospect of fewer jobs, lower incomes and the real possibility of being the first generation that will not do better economically than your parents.

My reason for sounding this somber note is not to discourage or scare you but to give you an appreciation of the obstacles you face in launching a successful career and to get your attention, at least long enough to share with you the three mission critical strategies that will help you launch a successful career and live an awesome life.

Who Am I and Why Should You Listen To Me?

I am a corporate trainer and coach on Personal Development, Communications, Leadership, Change Management and Stress Management and have helped thousands of people over the last 20 years in Australia, Britain, Canada and the United States increase their personal effectiveness and productivity. Perhaps most importantly, I am a parent whose son is presently going through the process of discovering who he is and what he wants to do with his life.

We have already invested a significant amount of money in his education and we would like to see a return on our investment. That return on investment (ROI) will be measured by his ability to establish and build a fulfilling and financially rewarding career and use that as the foundation to build real wealth and financial independence. Ultimately, I want for him what every parent wants for their children, which, in a nutshell, is for him to be healthy, wealthy, wise and happy; and by extension, to be a productive and compassionate member of society, leaving the world a better place than he found it.

Beyond my concern for my son's future, I am concerned about yours. Why should I be concerned about your future? I have to admit that there is some enlightened self interest here. Eventually, the cohort of your generation will be running the society when your parents and I have stepped off the stage into our retirement. Your generation will be producing the goods and services and paying the taxes that will fund our old age pensions and health care.

Our duty now is to ensure that you are equipped to assume the responsibilities that lie ahead of you and the better equipped you are with the tools, skills and sensibilities to take care of us in retirement the better off the cohort of your parents and I, known as the 'boomers' will be in our sunset years.

My Story

I've always had a keen interest in helping young people navigate the difficult and oftentimes treacherous passage from youth to adolescence and adulthood perhaps, because of the challenges and obstacles I faced in growing up.

I grew up on the gritty streets of Kingston, Jamaica. My father died when I was 15 years old. He was the sole breadwinner and unfortunately left us without a secure financial base or any prospects for the future. The burning question for me was how could I lift myself and help my siblings out of the dire straits we were left in? What did I have to do to find fulfillment and happiness? And so I embarked on what I now call my "Vision Quest".

This led me to the discovery of writers such as Shakespeare, Tolstoy, and Maugham, philosophers and thinkers such as Socrates and Gandhi, psychologists such as Carl Jung, Fritz Perls and Eric Berne, and the teachings of the Buddha and the Bhagavad Gita.

All pointed to living a life of passion, purpose, joy, happiness and fulfillment and offered their own blueprints for realizing this dream. I integrated and applied what I could from these mentors and sages and developed the discipline and determination to complete a Bachelor's degree in Journalism and Social Sciences from the University of the West Indies and a Master's in Communication Studies from the University of Windsor, in

Canada. I chose journalism and communication because I had a natural facility for writing and speaking, so the choice suited my gifts and talents.

However as motivated and driven as I was, I had pursued these degrees without a clear sense of what I would do on graduation. Should I go on to do my PhD? "It is a tough row to hoe", said my thesis advisor for my Masters. "Be prepared to invest another five years." I was exhausted and broke and didn't think I had another five years to give to academia.

I took the default route which was to return to Jamaica, justifying the decision that I would be in a position to "contribute" to the development of the society. I however had no idea what that meant. The most obvious fields where I could apply my skills would be in Journalism or Public Relations and Advertising. The problem was I had not cultivated any contacts in the field of Journalism, which in itself was limited. There were only two radio stations, one of which was publicly owned and a television station, also publicly owned; two newspapers, one private, the other partially owned by the government. Besides, I criticized the privately owned newspaper for the way it reported the news in my thesis, during a politically volatile period in Jamaica's development, and applying for a job there would have been awkward given the nature of my thesis.

I ended up in Public Relations and Advertising through a family contact who was well known as a journalist and public relations practitioner. But even though I was eminently qualified to work and succeed in that field, and did well enough, I had a disdain for spin and what I perceived then to be the lack of authenticity of the practitioners who pandered, as I saw it, to their clients, some of whom were their political masters. Eventually I began to garner some visibility along with the perception of being a political hack because of the organization I worked for and the position I held. Soon it became untenable to work in this context and so I returned to Canada.

On my return to Canada I landed a job in Community Development and Social Marketing promoting anti-drug and healthy lifestyle choices to public housing tenants but found their plight, the political and bureaucratic issues and the modest impact of the program discouraging.

This led me to the field of Training and Development when my wife brought my attention to a position for a seminar leader and trainer with a company that developed and facilitated seminars around the world. The position required good presentation and interpersonal communication skills, intellectual curiosity and flexibility, a desire to change and transform people's lives and a willingness to travel.

I knew I had found the career I wanted to pursue when 8:00 a.m. became 5:00 p.m. in a flash in the excitement and challenge of engaging participants in a seminar or workshop, and staying engaged and open to learning even as I shared what I knew. Best of all, was the real satisfaction of receiving feedback that I had indeed changed someone's life.

Since I've embarked on this career I've had the privilege of leading seminars and workshops in Australia, Britain, Canada and the United States on Communication, Leadership, Personal Development, Change Management, Stress Management and Facilitation Mastery for Teams and Training. This book is my latest effort to help college and university graduates save time, energy, money and tons of frustration launching a successful career by outlining the process I found through trial and error and at great personal and financial cost.

Lessons Learned

The point of all this is NOT to bore you with my story but to use it as a point of departure to share some lessons learned. So here are *a few* of the lessons I learned:

1. It is not enough to get a diploma or degree. You need to be clear about your direction in life, your mission and purpose and how this degree or diploma will serve this mission and purpose. Your mission and purpose is the overarching context within which you make your career choices.
2. You need to research the field and the industry your course of study leads to and determine the available opportunities. This includes finding and cultivating mentors and potential employers.
3. You also need to explore related fields and industries where you could profitably use the skills you gained from your course of study.
4. You need to be clear about these issues *before* you graduate. It's too late if you have no idea what your next steps are.

5. It is not only important to choose a course of study and a career that reflects your gifts and talents but it is also vital that what you do is congruent with your values and beliefs. I disdained what I perceived as public relations and advertising "spin" but found it fulfilling and worthwhile to use my communication skills in the seminars and workshops I conducted to inform, educate and help people transform their lives.

The Three Mission Critical Strategies

The rest of this book will go deeper into the three mission critical strategies I've alluded to. So what are these strategies? They are:
1. Clarify your Mission and Purpose. This is *your* Mission and *your* Purpose based on *your* own values, beliefs and talents and not the Mission and Purpose handed to you by Parents or Society.
2. Cultivate the Achiever's Mindset.
3. Execute the strategic Moves to achieve your dreams.

Clarify Your Mission and Purpose

In this chapter I want to discuss the importance of having a mission and purpose and take you through the process of creating a mission statement that reflects your values and beliefs and expresses your gifts and talents.

Many of us drift aimlessly through life without any sense of where we want to go, what we want to do or become and why. I've done seminars all over the world and have met many people who are unhappy with their jobs or their positions in life. They oftentimes see themselves as victims of circumstance, and are bitter and angry.

Whenever I meet unhappy, unfulfilled people I enquire whether they have a mission and purpose for their lives and invariably they don't. They live their life by default instead of by design and end up mired in frustration, failing to live up to a fraction of their potential.

Those who have a sense of what their mission and purpose is, oftentimes don't have a written mission statement that they use to guide their actions. Yet they intuitively know the value of having a mission and purpose and the importance of having a written one that they can use to track their journey. Those who have a written mission statement have more clarity, control, enthusiasm and optimism about their lives.

Stephen Covey, author of *The 7 Habits of Highly Effective People* notes that one of the principles to live by is to **Begin with the End in Mind**. To begin with the end in mind, according to Covey, is to begin with the image, picture, or paradigm of the end of your life as your frame of reference or criterion by which everything else is judged.

In that way you live in accordance with what is most important and meaningful to you. Beginning with the end in mind places your college or university career in context and opens you to exploring ways in which you can live your most awesome life.

Write Your Own Eulogy

An exercise that help you to begin with the end in mind is to write your own eulogy. This exercise may unnerve you but the aim of it is to give you the thirty thousand foot perspective or view. When we are young life seems to expand infinitely before us. We are healthy and energetic and have a feeling of immortality. And that's the problem, because whether or not we realize it, our life is flowing forward unceasingly and it is finite. Picture a hour glass with sand flowing from one glass into the other. The flow is ceaseless, night and day until the glass at the top is empty. The flow of the sand is analogous to the flow of your life. It is over too soon. So here is the exercise.

1. Imagine that you are at your funeral.

2. In attendance are family, friends, co-workers, members of your faith group or community organization.
3. What do these people have to say about you?
4. What kind of parent, spouse, family member, friend and co-worker were you?
5. What achievements and contributions have you made?
6. What difference has your life made to the people in the room and to the wider society?

Steve Jobs' Perspective

Steve Jobs was in the full flight of his life and career when he was diagnosed with pancreatic cancer in 2003 at age 49. The prognosis was grim but his doctors did the best they could and bought him some time. At one point he was told that it was in full remission and he could breathe a sigh of relief. However his sense of vulnerability never left him.

At his commencement speech to the 2005 class at Stanford University he said,

Remembering that I'll be dead soon is the most important tool I've ever encountered to help me make the big choices in life. Because almost everything — all external expectations, all pride, all fear of embarrassment or failure – these things just fall away in the face of death, leaving only what is truly important. Remembering that you are going to die is the best way I know to avoid the trap of thinking you have something to lose. You are already naked. There is no reason not to follow your heart.

In my own case I was confronted with my own mortality on four different occasions: each occasion was sudden, dramatic and alarming and left me with a sense that I needed to get on with living my life fearlessly and with urgency.

The BIG Questions

To gain clarity about your mission and purpose in life you have to confront and answer what I call the big questions. These are:

1. Who am I?
2. What am I doing here?
3. How am I going to live my life or spend my time while I am here?
4. What do I want to be remembered for, or what legacy do I want to leave behind?

These are not easy questions to answer. They take a lot of digging and soul searching but they are worth answering because the answers will help you gain clarity about your mission and purpose. So as best as you can, take some time now and answer these questions.

The Importance of a Personal Mission Statement

Here are the reasons why you need a personal mission statement. A personal mission statement…

1. Defines your purpose.
2. Puts your dreams into focus.

3. Gives you direction.
4. Gives you control over your life.
5. Is a standard against which you judge your success.

A Personal Mission statement helps you set your goals; what you want to do, be, have, and the kinds of experiences you would like to afford for yourself and the people you care about.

Bruce Lee's Personal Mission Statement

Here is an example of Bruce Lee's Mission Statement. It was written in January 1969. He titles his Mission Statement "My Definite Chief Aim" and it goes as follows:

"I Bruce Lee will be the first highest paid Oriental superstar in the United States. In return I'll give the most exciting performances and render the best of quality in the capacity of an actor. Starting 1970 I will achieve world fame and from then onward, till the end of 1980, I will have in my possession $10,000,000. I will live the way I please and achieve inner harmony and happiness."

He died on July 20, 1973. When he died he was reputed to be worth $10 million so he was ahead of the schedule he had set himself.

Oprah's Mission Statement
To be a teacher. And to be known for inspiring my students to be more than they thought they could be.

My Mission Statement
To be a source of light and joy to others, especially young people, inspiring them to be the best version of themselves by sharing the wisdom, knowledge, and understanding I've gained from my life experience as husband, father, teacher.

Mission Statements of Companies You Know
Companies are well aware of the importance of Mission Statements. Here are the Mission Statements of some well known companies.

Our vision is to be earth's most customer centric company; to build a place where people can come to find and discover anything they might want to buy online. Amazon

To bring inspiration and innovation to every athlete in the world. Nike

To create value and make a difference. Coca-Cola

How To Find Your Own Mission

The question now is how do you go about finding your own mission? Here is a process. You have to:

1. Know Yourself.
2. Clarify Your Values.
3. Clarify Your Beliefs.
4. Discover your Gifts.
5. Visualize the Life you want to Live.

Know Yourself

To know yourself you have to become aware of what makes you tick. Here are some questions you might start off with.

1. Am I generally outgoing, gregarious and friendly or am I self-contained and more of a thinker?
2. What are the key experiences that have shaped my outlook on life?
3. Am I an optimist or am I a pessimist?
4. What are the things I love to do and do well?
5. What are my strong religious or philosophical beliefs, if any?
6. What are my beliefs about how society should function?

Clarify Your Values

Your values are the ethical and moral principles that govern your life. Examples of values are compassion, honesty, fairness and kindness.

Reflect on Your Values

Nothing brings out the best and worst in people than money so here is a question for you. If you had more money than you could spend what would you do with your life? How would you spend your money? What causes would you support?

People such as Oprah and Bill Gates have used their vast wealth to improve the lives of people by building schools, giving scholarships, sponsoring research that will impact the health and well-being of individuals and the planet. On the other hand, others have used their wealth to indulge in self-destructive behavior, living profligate, dissolute lives. There is the story of the man in the U.S. who won a $300 million lottery. He thought he would express his love for his grand-daughter by giving her a weekly allowance of $2000. She blew the money on drugs with her boyfriend and both died of drug overdoses.

To compound the tragedy, the boyfriend's family blamed the man for enabling the self-destructive behavior of their son and brought a civil lawsuit against him. What seemed to all intents and purposes to be good fortune became the source for tragedy, all because of some questionable values. The man lamented that winning the lottery was the worst thing that could have happened to him as he inadvertently contributed to the death of his granddaughter, the most precious person for him in the world. He would have gladly given up the $300 million dollars to get back his grand-daughter.

Discover Your Gifts and Talents

Every one of us comes into this world with a set of gifts and talents that reflects our uniqueness and gives us the opportunity to make a contribution to the world. It is very important that your Mission Statement reflects your gifts and talents. Ironically most of us ignore or take our gifts and talents for granted. So how can you discover your gifts and talents?

Here are some questions you can ask yourself.

1. What are the things that I am endlessly fascinated about?
2. What subjects do I have to study to know more about the things I am fascinated about?
3. What are the things I like doing which come naturally to me?
4. What are my favorite subjects in school and what career would they lead to if I pursue them?
5. What are the gifts that my parents, guardians, teachers and friends say I have?

What is a Gift?

A gift is a talent or ability you're born with which enables you to do certain mental or physical activities effortlessly which others struggle with. A gift can also be referred to as a type of "smarts" or intelligence.

Researchers have found that there are many different forms of intelligence or "smarts" which are not measured by traditional IQ tests and that all of us are strong in at least one of these "smarts".

The Seven Types of Smarts

Dr. Howard Gardner, the Harvard researcher, developed the concept of multiple intelligences and identified the seven distinct ways we learn and know about reality. This classification of the seven types of "smarts" is based on his work. The seven types of "smarts" and the characteristics of people with these "smarts" are:

1. Music smarts.
2. Body smarts.
3. People smarts.
4. Self-smarts.
5. Picture smarts.
6. Word smarts.
7. Logic smarts.

Music Smarts

- People with Music Smarts have the ability to sing and use musical instruments.

- Can recognize and use rhythmic and tonal patterns.
- Become singers, composers, players in orchestras and bands and music teachers.
- Bob Marley is an example of someone with Music Smarts who was largely self-taught.

Body Smarts
- People with Body Smarts have the ability to execute activities that require excellent bodily control and coordination.
- Athletes, actors, professional dancers and mimes have highly developed Body Smarts.
- Usain Bolt, the world's fastest man, is an example of someone with Body Smarts.

People Smarts
- Those with People Smarts are good verbal and non-verbal communicators. They work well with others on teams or in groups.
- They can pick up on people's moods, temperaments and motivations and empathize with their feelings, fears, and beliefs.
- Counselors, teachers, therapists, religious leaders and politicians have highly developed People Smarts.
- Barack Obama is an example of someone with People Smarts.

Self Smarts
- People with Self Smarts are in touch with their moods, feelings and emotions.

- They can step back and observe themselves interacting with others and are aware of their impact.
- They can sense a connection to a reality that is larger than them and are aware of the wholeness of nature.
- Philosophers, psychiatrists, spiritual counselors and gurus have highly developed Self Smarts.
- The Dalai Lama is an example of someone with Self Smarts.

Picture Smarts

- People with Picture Smarts can see things in 3 dimensions.
- They have abilities to paint, draw, sculpt, navigate, make maps, and create architectural plans.
- Architects, graphic designers, map makers, industrial designers, painters and sculptors have highly developed Picture Smarts.
- Pablo Picasso is an example of someone with Picture Smarts.

Word Smarts

- People with Word Smarts are comfortable with language in its various forms.
- This includes storytelling, poetry, reading and writing, humor, symbolic thinking, grammar, metaphors, similes and abstract reasoning.
- Poets, playwrights, storytellers, novelists, public speakers and comedians have highly developed Word Smarts.

- J.K. Rowling, author of the *Harry Potter* novels is an example of someone with Word Smarts.

Logic Smarts
- People with Logic Smarts are great at math. They are comfortable with "scientific thinking" which draws logical conclusions or makes generalizations from sets of information.
- They can recognize patterns, work with numbers, and geometric shapes, and see relationships between separate and distinct pieces of information.
- Scientists, computer programmers, accountants, lawyers, bankers, and mathematicians all have Logic Smarts.
- Albert Einstein, is an example of someone with Logic Smarts.

EQ—Another Type of Smarts

Word Smarts and Logic Smarts are the only two types of intelligence that have been measured and valued as an indication of one's IQ. The emphasis in western education systems is on developing these two types of intelligence.

EQ or Emotional Intelligence is another type of smarts which is now regarded as perhaps even more important than IQ in predicting the probability of one's success. EQ is a combination of Self Smarts and People Smarts. It is said that whereas IQ gets you in the door of an organization, what distinguishes those who eventually make it to the executive suite is their possession of EQ.

EQ can be defined as "one's awareness of one's emotional states, the ability to effectively manage these states and to help others do the same for themselves." EQ is regarded as one of the most important smarts because it determines the quality of your relationships and hence your happiness. It makes sense that if you are self aware and know how to get along with others, you are likely to be happier.

What's Your Smarts?

As you read about the different types of "smarts" could you identify any that applied to you? On a scale of 1-10 where 1 is "none" and 10 is "gifted", where would you rate yourself in relation to these "smarts"? Has anyone ever complimented you for having one or a combination of these "smarts"?

Write Your Personal Mission Statement

You have just been taken through a process where you now should have most, if not all of the answers, to write a mission statement that reflects your values and beliefs and takes into consideration your gifts and talents. Review the answers to the questions and write your Mission Statement.

Writing your Personal Mission Statement is a major step on the road to realizing your dreams. Your Personal Mission Statement will help you to set the goals you need to achieve if you are to live your best life.

A Mission Statement for Everyone

I was taking my son Matthew, who may have been seven or eight years old at the time, to a soccer practice when out of the blue he asked, "Dad what must I do when I grow up?" He seemed to have given the question deep thought and so instead of rattling off a quick response such as "Lawyer" or "Doctor", which most parents want their kids to be, I paused for a moment to consider what I really wanted for him. Immediately I thought that what I really wanted for him was for him to be healthy, wealthy, wise and happy regardless of what he did in life and that was my response.

I think it is safe to say that we all want these for ourselves. They are all core goals that can be incorporated into our mission statement. Of course, to be healthy, wealthy, wise and happy probably means different things to different people and this is how I explained what I meant to him.

Health

Health is a basic and fundamental resource and includes physical, mental, emotional and spiritual health. To have physical health is to be free of ailments and to have enough energy and vitality to go about one's daily life with enough to spare. Physical health requires proper nutrition, exercise and sleep.

Mental health involves clear thinking, grounded in reality and logic. Emotional health is about having self-worth and self-esteem, being confident and comfortable in one's skin, and having a sense of loving connection to the world and others. Spiritual health is having a connection to a Higher Power however you define It.

Managing Stress

One of the most important things you can do to enhance your health is to learn how to manage stress. Stress, in and of itself, is not a bad thing. Dr. Hans Selye (1907-1982), the Canadian pioneer in stress research, defined it as "a non-specific response of the organism to any pressure or demand." My understanding of a "non-specific response" is that different people will have different responses when faced with the same situation. Some may laugh or cry; others may get angry or find deep reservoirs of calm capability.

People's responses to a stressor are determined by their perception of the stressor. A stressor that is perceived as threatening to the physical or emotional well-being of an individual will trigger what is called the fight or flight response. The fight or flight response is controlled by the old reptilian brain. To get a sense of the structure of the brain make a fist with your right hand, place it in the palm of your left hand and close your fingers around it. The palm of your left hand is the frontal lobe or neo-cortex. It functions as the executive and makes decisions based on logic and reason.

The right fist is the old reptilian brain which controls our survival instincts. The old reptilian brain contains the limbic system, which through the hypothalamus, controls the nervous system. The nervous system in turn controls blood pressure, heart rate, digestion. When a threat is perceived, the equivalent of a 911 emergency call is made to the nervous system and this triggers an alarm. At the alarm, the nervous system dumps adrenaline into the blood stream and the following reactions take place:

- The senses sharpen; the eyes dilate to let in maximum information and light.
- Heart rate and blood pressure increase.
- Breathing and metabolism increase.
- Blood is pumped to the arms and legs; clotting agents are released in the event of an injury.
- The digestive system shuts down and there is a cascade of emotions—anger, fear and fright throughout the system.

These natural reactions have not changed since the time we've been running from sabre toothed tigers and dinosaurs. They are hard-wired into the circuitry of our nervous systems and were appropriate for when we really needed to fight or flee to save our lives. We mobilized our energy and spent it appropriately.

The problem with living in modern society is that we are rarely in a life and death situation, but the same stress reactions are constantly being triggered by trivial issues such as sitting in traffic; waiting in line; being "dissed" by someone or having our belief systems and way of doing things challenged.

The constant triggering of the alarm buttons in our system results in hyper-arousal and eventually wears us down. We suffer *burn-out* and become prone to cancer, heart disease and high blood pressure, a few of the illnesses in which stress plays a part.

These diseases are major killers in North American society and are increasingly so for other cultures which adopt the stress laden North American lifestyle. It is therefore very important to become aware of how we are reacting to a situation and what is happening to us. Awareness lessens the severity of our reactions and hence our proneness to the diseases triggered by stress.

What I've just described is the typical negative reaction to stress. Researchers distinguish between good stress and bad stress. Good stress, also known as eustress, increases performance and efficiency. For example, Olympic athletes become Olympic champions because they are able to rise to the big moment and use the pressure they experience to perform well. They are able to get into a "flow" state which many describe as a focused and effortless state of peak performance.

Bad stress, also known as distress, robs us of our ability to cope effectively with the demands of our daily lives by taxing our physical, emotional, intellectual and spiritual resources. Again, using the Olympic athlete example, those who "choke" allow the pressure they feel to win, to get in the way of their performance.

The Relaxation Response

The Relaxation Response is the opposite of the stress reaction. It is the ability of the individual to bring the body/mind into a state of equilibrium and balance by lowering heart rate, breathing, blood pressure and metabolism through a controlled process of breath awareness, proper bodily posture and concentration of the mind.

The notion of the Relaxation Response was developed by Dr. Herbert Benson, Associate Professor of Medicine at the Harvard Medical School, who looked at the impact of stress on people and age old techniques in the East and West people used to mitigate the effects of the stress reaction. Since then, numerous studies have corroborated Dr. Benson's research that there is a capacity in human beings called the Relaxation Response and that it can be turned on at will, using certain techniques.

A Relaxation Response Exercise

Here is an exercise you can use to trigger the relaxation response when you are stressed.

- Sit up straight with feet firmly planted on the ground.
- Pull your shoulders up, tense them and let them drop naturally. Let your hands rest naturally in your lap.
- Close your eyes and allow your breath to flow naturally in and out of your nostrils. Do this for a few minutes and become aware of your bodily sensations.
- As you breathe in, experience the breath flowing into your nostrils, into your lungs; experience the rise and fall of your chest and your abdomen.
- With each inhalation, say in your mind, "I am breathing in relaxation and peace." With each exhalation say in your mind, "I am breathing out stress and tension."

- Do this for about five minutes. Record your experience.

    Return to this exercise when you experience stress and tension.

My Secret Strategy for Managing Stress

Earlier I mentioned that I had a difficult early life which sent me on a "Vision Quest" to find happiness and fulfillment as I was almost overwhelmed with anxiety and fear. On the quest I stumbled upon a book titled *The Three Pillars of Zen* written by Zen master Roshi Philip Kapleau, an American, who had gone to Japan on his own vision quest during a mid-life crisis, to find meaning and purpose. He spent thirteen years studying under the most distinguished masters of the day and became a pioneer in establishing Zen in the west teaching zazen.

Zazen is a form of meditation using the breath to focus attention and awareness, develop concentration and integrate body and mind. I began doing zazen and almost instantly began reaping the benefits. I had deep, dreamless, refreshing sleep and gradually the physical and emotional strain I felt subsided. My energy and concentration increased and I found that I could study better, longer and retain more. This gave me a competitive advantage over my peers in high school and university.

Zen meditation has become the staff that I lean upon when I need support. Over time I've become more and more capable of drawing on spiritual and emotional strength from within relying less and less on others for support. I've never had to use alcohol or drugs to cope with stress or to get high, unlike others I've known, who became dependent with harmful consequences for themselves and their families.

If you want to learn more on how you can use the breath to manage stress you can check out my program titled *Mastering Breath Awareness, An 'MBA' in Managing Stress* at www.MasteringBreathAwareness.com.

Wealth

To be wealthy is to have a certain measure of financial security, enough to exercise a certain amount of freedom and choice in one's life. It is important to make a distinction between wealth and income. Income is the salary you are paid on a weekly, monthly or annual basis for work that you do. Wealth are the assets that generate income for you. These assets would include investments in stocks, gold, jewellery and real estate. Those of us who are not born into wealth have to first earn the income to acquire the assets that will generate wealth.

Wealth is more than just money. It also means having deep, meaningful, loving and nurturing relationships. There are also other intangibles to wealth such as living in a society where there is freedom and liberty to pursue one's own personal happiness.

Wisdom

Wisdom is the capacity to integrate and apply the knowledge one gains from all available sources—rational, intuitive, emotional and practical—in elegant ways that affirms one's fundamental humanity and the humanity of others. It encompasses living with love, joy, compassion and equanimity.

Happiness

Happiness is a deep, open affirmation of "Yes!" to life and its myriad experiences. I always made the assumption that being healthy, wealthy and wise was enough but many philosophers and deep thinkers whom I regarded as wise weren't necessarily happy. Some of them became mired in deep despair and could have been considered as a little crazy.

Creating Your Vision Board

To remind yourself of your Mission and Purpose and keep it constantly in your consciousness you need to create a Vision Board. To create a Vision Board you will need the following:

- A sheet of Bristol board.
- A glue stick.
- A pair of scissors.
- Old newspapers, magazines and pictures.

Cut out and assemble pictures based on the following consideration:

- Imagine yourself living the life you ideally want to live 5, 10, 15 years from now?
- What job are you doing?
- What kind of house are you living in?
- What kind of car are you driving?
- What gifts and abilities are you using?
- Who benefits from those gifts and abilities?
- What experiences have you given yourself and your loved ones?

After you have assembled your Vision Board, put it in a prominent place where you can see it every day and let it inspire you to pursue your dreams.

Summary

We covered a lot in this chapter. I talked about the importance of having a clear mission and purpose; how a written mission statement gave Bruce Lee focus and direction and how companies use their mission statements to guide them.

I then outlined a five step process to help you find your own mission and purpose; discussed the seven types of Smarts; directed you to reflect on, and identify your dominant Smarts, which indicated what your gifts and talents were.

You were then asked to write a personal mission statement which reflected your gifts and talents, values and beliefs. I further suggested that your mission statement should be framed by a focus on health, wealth, wisdom and happiness as core principles.

You were then asked to create a vision board with images and pictures of your dreams and aspirations and put it in a prominent place to remind and motivate you to take action.

Cultivate the Achiever's Mindset

In this chapter we are going to look into how to cultivate the Achiever's Mindset and the elements that make up this Mindset. First, let us define the term "Mindset". The term "Mindset" refers to the whole superstructure of awareness, attitudes, beliefs, consciousness, mentality, and habitual thinking patterns that shape how we see ourselves in relation to the world. Mindset affects our self-confidence and self-esteem and in turn is affected by these qualities.

The Achiever's Mindset is an extraordinary mindset. It cuts through all fears and doubts like a diamond that cuts through everything but cannot be cut by anything. It is invincible and indomitable in its will to succeed. The Achiever's Mindset can also be described as "no limits" "possibility thinking" that supports us in "boldly going where no one has gone before", to quote the mission statement of the star ship *Enterprise* in the Star Trek series.

An example of this "no limits" "possibility thinking" was seen when President Kennedy announced and committed the United States in 1961 to the goal of putting a man on the moon and returning him safely to earth before the end of the decade. This feat was accomplished on July 20, 1969 when Neil Armstrong, the Apollo 11 Commander, stepped on the lunar surface with the immortal words,

"That's one small step for man, one giant leap for mankind."

When Kennedy made the announcement it was a paradigm shattering concept. Had the scientists and astronauts who were engaged in this endeavour questioned their abilities, or expressed doubt in achieving this goal we would probably still be earthbound wondering if it is possible. Today, we're talking about going to Mars or colonizing the moon or building cities in the ocean.

Another example of "no limits" "possibility thinking" which was breathtaking in its boldness and audacity was the decision of Barack Obama to run for President of the United States. Others would probably have talked themselves out of undertaking such a monumental task justifying this with the history of African Americans in the United States. Obama convinced Americans that he was the best candidate for the job and ran a brilliant campaign. On January 20, 2009 he became the first African American to be President of the United States.

What's Your Mindset?

So what's your Mindset? Interestingly if you place two glasses side by side half filled with water the question is, "are they half full or are they half empty?" Actually there's no physical difference between a glass that is half full and one that is half empty. The difference is perspective. Optimists see the glass as half full; pessimists see the glass as half empty. However from a psychological perspective it is easier to fill a glass that is half full than it is to fill a glass that is half empty.

Elements of the Achiever's Mindset

Let's now take a look at the elements of the Achiever's Mindset. There are three elements that make up the Achiever's Mindset. These are:

1. Positive Attitudes.
2. Supportive Beliefs.
3. Positive Self Esteem and Self Confidence.

What are Attitudes?

Attitudes are the thoughts and feelings we have about ourselves and the world, and the way we communicate these through our behavior. Attitudes can be right or wrong, positive or negative. The right attitude is one that helps us accomplish our goals and dreams, assuming that those goals and dreams are ethical, legal and moral.

According to Charles Swindoll, author, educator and preacher "Attitude is more important than facts. It is more important than the past, than education, than money, than circumstances, than failures and successes, than what other people think, or say or do. It is more important than appearance, ability or skill."

Signs of a Positive Attitude

Someone with a positive attitude would have the following behaviors:
- Energetic
- Cooperative

- Smiling
- Sense of humor
- Happy
- Problem solver; focused on 'can do'

Signs of a Negative Attitude
Someone with a negative attitude would be:
- Lethargic
- Uncooperative
- Scowling
- Serious; gloomy
- Depressed
- A whiner; complainer; focused on 'can't'

What are Supportive Beliefs?
Supportive beliefs are the ideas, assumptions, and opinions we have of ourselves that nurture and support us in the achievement of our goals. An example of a supportive belief is, "I am smart and capable and can harness all my resources to achieve my goals."

The Importance of Positive Self Esteem
Talk show host, Oprah Winfrey, in her final show closing out 25 years of transforming people's lives, noted that the common thread that was at the root of all the issues guests on her show struggled with, whether it was addiction, anxiety, or not stepping into their greatness was a sense of being unworthy.

She emphatically told her audience that they were enough; that the fact that they were born and are living on this earth here, now, is testament to their worthiness and all they had to do was to listen for the life that they were called to live. This is the message that all the great sages and philosophers have been delivering from time immemorial—that the capacity for greatness lies within all of us and to be truly worthy is simply to acknowledge this capacity and allow it to guide us.

For many of us that is easier said than done. In the process of being socialized into the norms and values of a society many powerful forces act upon us, often unconsciously, that shape our self esteem.

Interestingly, according to psychologists, the minds of newborn infants are like blank sheets of paper. They have no concept of a self separate and apart from the world, nor do they have a self concept. They don't know whether they are male or female, rich or poor, black or white. As they grow and develop and begin to interact with the world they begin to learn about themselves, their roles and where they fit in the society. Society becomes their social mirror. What they learn about themselves shape their self concept. Their self concept shapes their self esteem and their self esteem in turn impacts their self confidence.

The Forces That Shape Our Self Esteem and Self Confidence

To *"esteem"* someone according to the *Collins English Dictionary*, is to have great respect or regard for that person. Self-esteem can thus be defined as the respect, regard or attitude one has for oneself. The dictionary defines self-confidence as belief in one's own abilities or self assurance. Self esteem and self confidence can be high or low, positive or negative.

So what are the forces that play such an important role in our self-esteem? The most important forces that shape our self-esteem are:

- Parents.
- Teachers.
- Friends.
- Media.
- Religious institutions.

The Impact of Parents

Our parents have the earliest impact on our sense of worthiness. This is communicated in what they said to us, and how they treated us physically. Were they attentive and responsive to our needs? Were they encouraging in the things they said to us as we explored and learned about our world? Or were they critical and communicated their lack of confidence in us to rise to the challenges all of us are destined to face in our lives.

Dr Eric Berne, author of *What Do You Say After You Say Hello?* and the founder of the psychological approach to human dynamics called *Transactional Analysis* notes that just the setting for one's conception was an important factor in one's life. Did our parents have a loving, respectful and stable relationship? Did they look forward to our conception and birth or did they regard our conception as a mistake? And where were they in their own development as individuals when they became parents? Were they emotionally and financially stable or were they still struggling to find themselves and their way in the world? All of these were factors which impacted how you were treated as a child.

More often than not, most people, including our parents function in default mode and oftentimes are oblivious to the impact their words and actions have on their children. Later on I will give you some tools to raise your self-awareness and rebuild your self-esteem and self-confidence.

The Impact of Teachers

Our teachers are the next set of important people in our lives. Many of us can remember a teacher who played a pivotal role in our lives in encouraging and inspiring us to strive for excellence and who became role models. I was fortunate to attend a high school, a rare privilege in Jamaican society, which had a culture of high expectation for its students. We were all expected to go on to university, get a profession and become productive members of society.

I remember and am grateful to those teachers who set high expectations, coached us on our strengths, helped us address our weaknesses, modeled passion and purpose, and exhorted us to live upright, productive lives. There were also teachers who were not very skillful in getting the best out of their students resorting instead to sarcasm, detentions and corporal punishment. Those teachers were despised and feared and it was never too soon or early to drop their courses or leave their classes. Our distaste for them was often reflected in poor grades.

The Impact of Friends

As we grew older and entered our teenage and young adult years our friends played a more important role in our lives than our parents and teachers. They reinforced us in our identities or helped us develop new identities. Some of us may have become part of a popular in-group and enjoyed the status of "first among equals", while others, for various reasons were regarded as outcast, teased, bullied and called names.

The Impact of Media

As we engaged the wider society and started to consume popular culture through the mass and social media we began to be aware of images, popular beliefs and stereotypes about our cultural groups, socio-economic backgrounds, gender, and sexual orientation. Based on what we picked up, we began to form opinions about ourselves and others. Where did people like us fit in society? Were we o.k. or not o.k.? Were we portrayed positively or negatively? Did we see positive role models, people that looked like us with the same backgrounds in the media?

The Impact of Religious Institutions

Our religious institutions also played a significant role in our concept of ourselves. I grew up in a fundamentalist Christian context which shaped my early notions of the nature of man, the character of women, temptation, the devil and sex based on the story of Adam and Eve. These are concepts and ideas that one has to grapple with as one develops a philosophy grounded in reality and reason.

What did you learn from your tradition about the nature of man and the character of women? And what did you learn about God? Was He a jealous, vengeance seeking old guy or was She a loving and compassionate mother? And what were you taught about other people who practiced religious and sacred paths that were different from yours?

Questions We Should Ask Ourselves

The questions raised are all very powerful questions that will give you vital clues on the impact these people and institutions had on your self-esteem and self-confidence.

Socrates, the great philosopher from ancient Greece said, "The unexamined life is not worth living" and spent his entire life in pursuit of wisdom and understanding by asking questions and engaging others in conversations that peeled away their unexamined assumptions and beliefs. When we start to examine our concepts of ourselves, our beliefs and how we acquired them, we see that many or most of them were taught to us; that we were like clean sheets of paper that the people and institutions mentioned wrote *their* narratives on.

The net effect these people and institutions have on us is that we come into adulthood having a positive or negative concept of ourselves which in turn affect our self-esteem and self-confidence.

How we function in the world as adults depends very much on whether we have high or low self esteem and so it is very important that we develop a self reflective process that enables us to unearth and question what we have been taught about ourselves, and ultimately to shape and redefine who we are in a way that serves our positive growth and development as human beings. So take some time and answer the questions we raised and the following:

1. How have the people and institutions we mentioned affected your self-esteem.
2. What are the positive things they have said and done that have built your self-esteem?
3. What are the negative things they have said and done that have diminished your self-esteem?
4. How would you defend yourself against the negative comments of these people and institutions?

Building Positive Self Esteem

One of the great things about us as human beings is that we can adapt and change. We can literally erase the old program and re-program ourselves for success. Self-awareness is the basis for any kind of change and asking yourself the questions I suggested and answering them is the first step in building positive self-esteem. There are other steps in the process. These are:

1. Practicing positive self talk
2. Practicing positive affirmations
3. Practicing positive visualizations
4. Creating an Achievement Log
5. Failing your way to Success

6. Directing Loving-kindness to yourself and others

Practicing Positive Self Talk

People with poor self-esteem invariably engage in negative self talk. Oftentimes their negative self-talk is the unconscious replay of the negative things they heard about themselves from their parents, teachers, friends, and significant institutions such as media.

Jack Canfield, author of the *Chicken Soup for the Soul* series of books, focused on the development of self-esteem in his early work and got people to consider the impact of their self-talk on themselves by asking the question, "If I spoke to my best friend the way I talk to myself, would my best friend remain my best friend?"

This question forced me to pay attention to my self-talk and I became aware of how I berated myself in the same way my parents berated me when I was clumsy or failed to live up to their expectations. The words and tone they used were the same words and tone I used and I would end up feeling awful. So reflect on your self-talk and ask yourself the following questions:

1. What are the words you use to describe yourself?
2. What is more dominant for you? Positive self-talk or negative self-talk?
3. What are the positive things you say to yourself?

4. What are the negative things you say to yourself?
5. Reflect on your inner voice. Does it remind you of anyone?
6. How does it make you feel about yourself?

Brag like Muhammad Ali

People of my generation were captivated by an African-American boxer by the name of Muhammad Ali who burst upon the scene in the 1960s. His dazzling foot-speed and lightning fast hands were only matched by his ability to brag about his abilities and put down his opponents.

He would punctuate his speech with the declaration "I am the Greatest!" Such a declaration was stunning in its swagger and cockiness, especially at a time when blacks in the United States were barely regarded as second class citizens. At best it would subject him to scorn, ridicule and contempt and at worst, it would set the white establishment against him, which it did, when he refused to be drafted into the US Army.

To get a sense of who he was, go to You Tube or Google "Muhammad Ali Greatest Speech." Observe his swagger, his tone, his words. Pretend that you have been asked to play him as a character and as best as you can become him in tone and attitude.

- After you think you can imitate Muhammad Ali close your eyes, take a few deep breaths, exhale and relax.

- Now think of something about yourself that you really like and admire. Get really high on yourself!
- Write about yourself in glowing and admirable terms. Compose it as a rap or poem.
- Stand in front of a full length mirror and as energetically and emphatically as possible recite your poem about yourself. How did that feel?
- If you can summon the courage to recite it in front of a live audience—family or friends, that would be even better.
- If you were unable to do the exercise, what is holding you back?

Practicing Positive Affirmations

Another way to improve self-talk and self-esteem is to create positive affirmations. Positive affirmations are positive personal statements made about one's self in the present tense. An example of a positive affirmation is the one created by Emile Coué, the famous French psychotherapist, "Everyday in every way I get better and better." Affirmations are not necessarily true at the time you make them. They are instead expressions of what you would be if you became your ideal self. Positive affirmations reinforce positive attitudes and behavior.

How to Create Positive Affirmations

- Close your eyes. Take a few deep breaths. Exhale and relax.
- Think of five things you like about yourself or five qualities or skills you would like to develop.

- Write them down.
- Turn the statements you have written down into affirmations.
- Share your affirmations with someone who is close to you and supportive.

Practicing Positive Visualizations

Visualization is another powerful technique you can use to feel better about yourself. Positive visualization is the use of your imagination in a positive way to paint a better picture of yourself or your situation. Visualizations are powerful because the unconscious mind does not distinguish between an imaginary and a real event.

Elite athletes and other high achievers use this technique to complement their preparation for their events. They visualize themselves being calm and relaxed, winning their events, or performing at a very high level and soaking up the accolades of the crowd. When they actually perform in their events they are not anxious and fearful because as far as their unconscious mind is concerned, they have won this event several times over.

Emile Coué, the French psychotherapist mentioned earlier, confirmed the power of visualization when he said, "When the imagination and the willpower are in conflict, are antagonistic, it is always the imagination that wins, without any exception. When the imagination and the willpower are harmoniously pulling in the same direction, irresistible force is the result."

The Power of Visualization

This exercise should demonstrate the power of visualization to you. You may want to work with someone who will read out the following instructions to you. The person reading the instructions should give you enough time to clearly visualize each step before moving on. You could also record the instructions and play them back.

- Close your eyes, take a deep breath and exhale, breathing out all your tensions.
- See yourself sitting at your dining table.
- On the table is a basket of fresh lemons.
- See the colors...smell them.
- Get a knife, take one of the lemons out of the basket and cut it.
- Take one half of the lemon and squeeze the juice on your tongue.
- Let the juice run back into your throat.
- Now come back into the room.

What happened as you visualized squeezing the lemon juice onto your tongue? The response of people who do this visualization exercise is that they find themselves making saliva as they imagine the tartness of the lemon juice running into the back of their throats.

The next time you know that you will be required to perform at a level where the stakes are high at a personal and professional level do what elite athletes do. Use your imagination to visualize yourself performing well. Make it as vivid as possible by engaging all your senses.

What do you see, hear, and feel? Are you calm, relaxed, in control? Can you see yourself as the greatest in this situation? Run the scene over and over in your mind until you can confidently say "yes!" to all the questions I asked and you are eager and enthusiastic to go out and "knock their socks off!" as the saying goes.

The Essence of High Self Esteem

The essence of high self-esteem, according to Jack Canfield, is knowing that you are capable and lovable. To be capable is to have the ability, competence, resources and skills to be successful in whatever you set out to do. To be lovable is to be attractive and worthy of love. How do you know whether you're capable and lovable? Here is an exercise that will help you determine how capable and lovable you are.

The Capable and Lovable Exercise[1]

- Get a piece of paper and divide it into two columns.
- Label one column "Capable" and the other "Lovable."
- In the "Capable" column list the things you do well.
- In the "Lovable" column list the qualities that make you a lovable person.
- Try to fill both columns with as many abilities and skills that confirm that you are a capable and lovable person.
- Aim for at least 20 skills and qualities respectively.
- Give yourself a treat if you were able to do so.

---

[1] Adapted from Jack Canfield's *How to Build High Self-Esteem*

- If you were not able to do so ask friends, family, colleagues for their feedback.
- Keep adding to the columns.

This exercise should prove that you are indeed capable and lovable in many ways. You ought to begin feeling better about yourself as you confirm that you are capable and lovable.

Creating Your Achievement Log

Another activity you can do to build your self-confidence and self-esteem is to create an Achievement Log. Your Achievement Log is a diary of your triumphs. It is a running score of all the things you have tried and succeeded at. It becomes a bank of stored successes and warm and fuzzy feelings that you can draw upon when you want to remind yourself that you are an achiever or when you want to shore up your self-confidence. Here is what you need to do to create an achievement log.

- Purchase a notebook and label it "My Achievement Log."
- List the things you've achieved that you're proud of.
- Write the date when you had your achievement, the reaction of others and how you felt.
- It is o.k. if you cannot remember the date. Just add the achievements to your log.
- Keep adding to your Achievement Log until you've built up a rich bank of achievements that you can draw on when you need to.

Failing Your Way To Success

As mentioned before, self-esteem and self-confidence are very closely related and mentioned in the same breath. Self-confidence comes from a sense of competence and capability. Competence and capability are built from doing, gaining experience and expertise. To gain experience and expertise you have to take risks. Many people hold themselves back because of their fear of failure. However, the people I've known who have succeeded spectacularly also have failed more than others.

Years ago, a seminar leader colleague of mine declared triumphantly that he was failing his way to success and the statement initially baffled me until I grasped the truth of the paradox of failure. Failure is not failure if the attitude you bring to it is that it is not a judgment of you or your abilities but rather important feedback. There is the popular story of Thomas Edison, the inventor of the light bulb, who apparently conducted thousands of trials before he got it right. He never considered any of the experiments he conducted failures. They were results. He is reported to have said in relation to his efforts to invent the light bulb that "If I find 10,000 ways something won't work, I haven't failed. I am not discouraged, because every wrong attempt discarded is another step forward."

Michael Jordan, said to be one of the greatest basketball players of all time, said of his failures, "I've missed more than 9,000 shots in my career...I've lost almost 300 games...26 times I've been trusted to take the game winning shot and missed...I've failed over and over and over again in my life...And that is why I succeed."

Directing Loving-kindness to Yourself

Earlier I said that people with poor self-esteem oftentimes unconsciously internalize the criticisms and negative comments made to them by parents, teachers, friends, media and religious institutions. These criticisms and negative comments become part of what I call their Inner Critic. The Inner Critic is harsh and unforgiving and continually beats up on them. The Inner Critic robs them of the crucial elements of high self-esteem—feeling capable and lovable.

Directing loving-kindness to yourself is a gentle and deliberate way of dissolving the harshness of the Inner Critic. Loving-kindness meditation was a practice that the Buddha taught his monks. The Buddha is reputed to have said to his monks, "Of all the people in the entire Universe who is worthy of your love, none is more worthy than you." From an inner psychological perspective, directing loving-kindness to yourself is the equivalent of replacing the Inner Critic with a gentler, kinder person and that person is You.

Loving-kindness begins with a deep appreciation of one's self and one's basic goodness as a human being. Loving-kindness replaces mindless, negative self-talk with conscious, positive affirmations directed toward ourselves and then to others. Affirmations, as we noted earlier, are strong, positive statements about one's self in the present tense. Affirmations help to reinforce positive attitudes and behaviours. Examples of affirmations are, "I am a great stress manager; I have all the tools I need to live a good life; I am free of anger and hatred; I am filled with compassion and joy; I like and appreciate myself."

To begin practicing loving-kindness, stabilize and ground yourself by focusing on your breath and as you breathe in count "one" and as you breathe out count "two". Continue in this manner all the way up to ten. When you feel calm and relaxed repeat the above affirmations, or ones you create, silently to yourself, absorbing yourself in the goodwill and generous feelings that arise out of these affirmations. Direct these feelings to yourself, saying, "May I be well, may I be happy, may I be free from stress and anxiety, may I be free from anger and hatred, may I be full of generosity and goodwill towards myself and others."

You will probably find it challenging to direct loving-kindness to yourself in the beginning. Most people find it challenging because our early socialization equate loving ourselves with being selfish, self-involved, egotistic and narcissistic. The truth is that you cannot give what you don't have, and if you don't love yourself and take care of yourself, you won't be able to love others.

To love yourself is to esteem or hold yourself in high regard. Holding yourself in high regard does not mean that you put others down. All it means is that you wish the best for yourself, and in wishing the best for yourself, you wish it also for others.

Summary

In this chapter you were introduced to the concept of the Achiever's Mindset. We explored elements of the Achiever's Mindset which we said were:

1. Positive attitudes

2. Supportive beliefs
3. Positive self-esteem

You were then given a blue-print or road map for developing positive self-esteem, even if, like so many others, your self-esteem was damaged in your interactions with the significant people and institutions in your life during your formative years. To develop positive self-esteem you need to:

1. Practice positive self-talk.
2. Practice positive affirmations.
3. Practice positive visualizations.
4. Create an achievement log.
5. Fail your way to success.
6. Direct loving-kindness to yourself and others.

Thus far you have been taken through a process, whether you realize it or not, to master the inner game of success and achievement. In the next chapter I'll take you through the process of mastering the outer game of success and achievement by outlining the strategic moves you need to make to launch a successful career.

The Four Strategic Moves

In this chapter we'll examine the four strategic moves you need to make to launch a successful career. These are:

1. How to market and position yourself in the job market and the communication skills you need to do so.
2. How to find a mentor and a coach.
3. Developing the entrepreneur's mindset and applying it to your career.
4. Mastering the money game.

Ideally these are moves you should have been making throughout the course of your college or university career and not at the last minute when you are on the verge of graduating. The Chinese proverb that the best time to plant a tree was 20 years ago and the next best time is now, applies here. Throughout the course of your career and your life the best strategy to execute is a proactive strategy, so let's take a look at what it means to be "proactive".

The *Collins English Dictionary* defines "proactive" as "tending to initiate change rather than reacting to events." Wayne Gretzky, the Canadian hockey legend, demonstrated how to be proactive in the way he played the game and probably explains why he was so successful. His approach to the game, he said, was knowing where the puck was going to be before it got there, and positioning himself to meet it when it arrived.

The opposite of being "proactive" is to be "reactive", so let's compare the difference between proactive and reactive people.

Proactive People	*Reactive People*
Act	React
Take Responsibility	Blame Circumstances
Exercise Choice	Accept Powerlessness
Are Problem Solvers	Are the Problem
Positive	Negative
Optimists	Pessimists
Focus on controlling themselves	Focus on manipulating others

So before going any further what are some of the proactive strategies you could take *before* graduating? Here are a few.

1. Begin networking. It's never too early or too late to begin.
2. Schedule fact finding interviews with experts in your field and people you want to work with.
3. Volunteer to gain practical skills and build your résumé.

Strategic Move #1 Market and Position Yourself

Marketing and positioning yourself is a critical strategic move. Marketing is a process of making yourself attractive and gaining attention in the marketplace.

Positioning is carving out a unique place in the marketplace relative to your competition that will leave a lasting, favorable and advantageous impression on your potential employer.

You Incorporated

One of the ways in which you can position yourself to stand out from the many people you are competing with is to see yourself as a corporate entity vying to win a valuable contract with the company you want to work with. That is a very empowering position to take because most people going into the marketplace see themselves essentially as an employee with very little bargaining power.

Now suppose you saw yourself as the President and CEO of 'You Incorporated' and positioned yourself as an independent consultant to the company you choose to work with, with the mission to increase and add value to that company, what would you do to get the contract or be hired? Do you see how this positioning immediately puts you in a proactive, problem solving mode? Instead of looking for a job you are approaching this company like a consultant.

The Consultant's Approach

As a consultant you would have researched the industry that this company is a part of, bearing in mind the following questions:

1. What are the issues peculiar to that industry?
2. What are the unique challenges of the company you want to work with?
3. What keeps the CEO or your potential boss awake at nights?
4. What solutions and ideas do you have that can help the company or your prospective boss solve their most pressing problems?

Notice how these questions switch you into a proactive mode where your concern is what you can do for the company you choose to work with rather than what they can do for you. Notice also the distinction between working *for* as opposed to working *with* an organization.

The answer to question four will differentiate you from the competition and help to define your Unique Selling Proposition.

What's Your Unique Selling Proposition (USP)?

In marketing terms a unique selling proposition is what differentiates a product or service from its competitors in the marketplace and thus gives it a competitive advantage. So to establish your USP you have to demonstrate to the company you have chosen to work with that you are not merely a job seeker but a value-added asset. You have to establish that you're a proactive, creative problem solver. To determine your USP you have to answer the following questions:

1. Why should the company you're applying to, hire you instead of the thousands of other graduates with the same degrees or diplomas who are entering the marketplace?
2. What differentiates you from them?
3. What can you do, or have done to differentiate yourself from the competition?

A unique selling proposition more often than not comes with a solid guarantee. A mentor of mine who developed his expertise in the trade show niche had a simple USP that said "Crowds Guaranteed". He would go to a convention in Las Vegas and approach a company offering his services for free to bring crowds of people to their booths.

He would then go into action and get the guaranteed crowds to the booths. When he secured the attention and interest of the company he made them an offer they couldn't refuse. If they wanted him to continue bringing crowds to the booth they would have to pay him a certain fee or risk him taking his services to their competitor. He would then set a mutually agreed upon performance standard which, if he met and exceeded, would net his fee *plus* a commission based on the value of conversions from prospects to clients.

He said he has never had to formally apply for a job and has always been in a position to choose who he works *with*. He is the one who made the distinction between working *for* and working *with* a company. You work for an employer; you work with a client. So here is a question for you, "How much of an impact would you make if you made a guaranteed performance offer to a company where they would pay you based on results and instead of taking a salary you negotiate a fee with a commission for exceeding results?" Would that approach differentiate you from being a job seeker?

Develop Effective Communication Skills

To market yourself effectively you have to learn how to communicate effectively. Communicating effectively allows you to:

1. Build relationships.
2. Work on teams.
3. Resolve challenging interpersonal conflicts.
4. Inspire and persuade bosses, colleagues and customers to invest in your ideas or buy your services.

The most important ways in which people communicate are Writing, Public Speaking and Presentation, and Interpersonal interactions. Whatever your mode of communication all forms of communication involves a certain process which I've outlined below.

The Communication Process

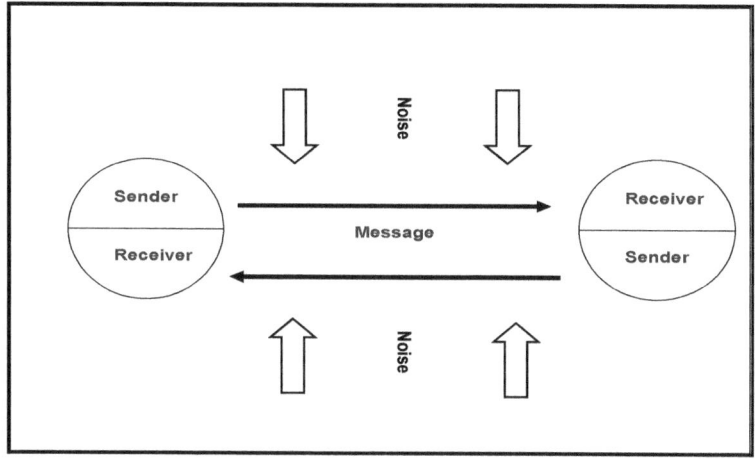

As the diagram shows, in every communication process there is a source, a message, a receiver and a channel through which the message is communicated. Harold Lasswell, a noted communication scholar, summarized the communication process in the following formula as:

Who says **What** to **Whom** over what **Channel** with what **Effect**. The diagram shows the sender (**Who**) transmitting the message (**What**) to the receiver (**Whom**). Every message is sent with the intention to get a response or effect.

As the diagram shows, 'noise' impinges on all aspects of the communication process. Noise can be described as anything which interferes with the sending and reception of a message. Noise can be external or internal.

Types of Communication Noise

There are six types of communication noise that interfere with the transmission of your messages. These are:
1. **Environmental noise** – e.g. the sounds of sirens close by or a blaring radio that prevents you from hearing what is being said.
2. **Mental noise** – e.g. your values and beliefs that clash with the values and beliefs of the other. Both parties fall back into a defensive mode rather than staying open to hear, understand and explore what each other is saying. The other mental noise is the intrusion of your own thoughts even as the other person is communicating to you.
3. **Emotional noise** – e.g. anger and fear. These emotions are huge obstacles in the way of effective communication. They trigger more of a flight/fight response rather than a desire or ability to communicate rationally and logically.
4. **Social noise**– e.g. bias, prejudice, dislike. We are disinclined to give people an opportunity to share their point of view if we don't like or have a bias against them.
5. **Disorganized message**. Awkward expressions and unskillful grammar and punctuation can make it difficult to understand a message.

6. **The use of Words and their meanings in popular culture.** Different generations have different meanings for words. When I was growing up, if something was very good it was described as 'bad' by the hip, young people of my generation. The first time I heard a 'Gen Xer' describe someone as 'sick', I thought that the person they were referring to was not well, only to realize that they meant that the person was 'amazing'!

The Importance of First Impressions

A very important aspect of the communications process is the impression you make on a person when you meet them for the first time. As the saying goes, "You never get a second chance to make a first impression." First impressions are important because people judge and are judged on first impressions. First impressions can either open or close doors of opportunity depending on the context you're in.

How To Make Your Best First Impression

How can you ensure that you make your best first impression all the time? The following are some guidelines.
1. Pay attention to your appearance (clothes, grooming, posture, gestures, and facial expressions).
2. Pay attention to how you sound (voice quality, volume, tone, rate, and the confidence it conveys).

3. Pay attention to what you say (vocabulary, grammar, how informed you are).
4. Listen actively. It is said that the best conversationalists aren't the people who dominate a conversation with their own views, but the people who listen actively and make a genuine attempt to understand the other person by asking questions and seeking to clarify their understanding by paraphrasing the person they are communicating with.

How To Impress At Your Job Interview

Perhaps the context where making your best first impression matters most is going for a job interview. When going for a job interview you need to follow these six guidelines:

1. Wear clean, well pressed clothes and polished shoes. Men should wear a black suit, white shirt and a solid tie. Women should wear a pair of closed medium height shoes or pumps, dark skirt that go just below the knee with a high collar blouse and matching jacket. The overall aim as a woman is to appear businesslike and professional.
2. Pay close attention to grooming, especially hair, teeth, nails and skin.
3. Know why you want the job and be able to articulate this well.
4. Be able to say how you will bring value to the employer and why you are the best candidate for the job.

5. Listen very carefully to questions and ask the interviewer(s) to repeat or clarify their questions if you don't quite understand what they are asking.
6. Be prepared to give specific examples of times you demonstrated leadership, interpersonal communication, problem solving skills and initiative to get superior results. These are the behaviors employers want to know you will demonstrate on the job.

The Importance of Social Media

Social media is a tool that can leave a lasting and indelible first impression of you. Potential employers will most likely check out your profile on social media to determine how well you would fit in with their organization. Whatever you say or post on the internet never dies so be very careful what you say.

In the 2015 Canadian Federal elections candidates from all three political parties were dropped by their parties for things they said and did, oftentimes years earlier, when some of them were teens, which were embarrassing to themselves and the parties they represented. Appearing nude or drunk on camera; making profanity laced, bigoted statements or anything that calls into question your judgment or character are all career killers.

How We Communicate

Earlier I said that the most important ways in which we communicate are by Writing, Speaking, which involves Public Speaking and Presentation, and Interpersonal interactions. Let's take a look at Public Speaking and Interpersonal interactions.

Effective Public Speaking

The people at the top of their fields are invariably masters at public speaking. It is said that speaking in public ranks number one among the top ten human fears as follows:

1. Speaking before a group
2. Heights
3. Insects and bugs
4. Financial problems
5. Deep water
6. Sickness
7. Death
8. Flying
9. Loneliness
10. Dogs

Comedians like to point out that the person who is doing the eulogy at someone's funeral would prefer to be in the casket. Here are some of the reasons why people fear speaking in public.

- Fear of failure
- Fear of ridicule
- Fear of rejection
- Embarrassment or loss of face
- Judgment from the audience
- Imagining the worst

How to Overcome the Fear of Public Speaking

The self-esteem and self-confidence boosting exercises for cultivating the Achiever's Mindset can help you overcome this fear. There is nothing wrong with feeling a little nervous before giving a presentation. That arousal will put a little adrenaline in your system and give you the energy to be compelling and engaging. The old advice is to make the butterflies you feel in your stomach fly in formation.

Here are some other ways to overcome the fear of public speaking:

- Know and prepare your topic very well, especially the introduction, as you are more inclined to be nervous during the beginning of your presentation.
- Know your audience very well; what makes them tick; the problems and issues they are grappling with.
- Be clear about your purpose. How will your presentation solve their problem or benefit them. Do you want to inform, educate, or entertain?
- Be clear about the actions you want your audience to take and ask them to do so.

- Be confident that what you're offering is a gift that will inspire and save them time, energy, and money; improve their relationships or contribute massively to their personal development and effectiveness, and have proof that this is so.
- Take care of yourself; be well rested and nourished.
- Dress comfortably and appropriately to enhance your self esteem and self confidence.
- Evoke the Relaxation Response through deep breathing.
- Take your time. Pause.
- Be familiar and comfortable with the technology you're using, having in place backup systems—computers, batteries, lamps, bulbs, data storage in case something goes wrong.

How to Improve Interpersonal Interactions

Unskillful interpersonal interactions oftentimes lead to conflict and so the aim in interpersonal interaction is to promote understanding and goodwill. To promote understanding and goodwill, Stephen Covey recommends that we seek first to understand, then to be understood.

In seeking to first understand, one of the most important communication skills one can master is empathic listening. Empathic listening involves:

- Listening to get inside the other person's frame of reference and understand their point of view.
- Listening with your ears for tone and how something is said, and with your eyes and heart to

pick up non-verbal cues as well as what is *not* being said.
- Withholding judgment.
- Allowing the other person to speak without interruption.

According to Covey, the greatest compliment you can pay, and the best way to validate someone, is to listen to them with the sole intention of understanding them.

The Principle of Win/Win

Another powerful principle that you can use to govern your relationship with others is the principle of win/win. In a win/win relationship people seek only what is beneficial to everyone in the relationship. They play fair and are respectful of the feelings and wishes of each other. Where there are differences, they cooperate to resolve them in a way that leaves everyone satisfied with the decision.

His commitment to this principle helped Covey facilitate a complex and difficult negotiation where lots of money and prestige were at stake and where one-upmanship characterized the relationship prior to him coming in as a facilitator. By setting that principle as a ground rule for negotiations and by pledging that, "I don't win, if you don't win", he was able to get people to work together as collaborators to resolve their differences rather than as advocates seeking the best advantage for one side.

Managing Conflict

However much we may try to avoid conflict, chances are that some interactions will deteriorate and when that happens we ought to know how to manage conflict with grace and ease. Here are some steps you can take to do so:

- Stay calm; stay centered.
- Breathe deeply.
- Listen carefully; don't interrupt.
- Acknowledge the other person's point of view.
- State your point of view clearly.
- Seek win/win solutions.
- Don't blame.
- Speak in a calm, even tone.
- Play fair.
- Honour agreements.

Strategic Move #2 Find a Mentor or Coach

It is very important to find a mentor or coach who can help you become established in your field. A mentor or coach is someone who has the knowledge, skills, experience and relationships in a field who is willing to share those assets with you. They can take you to the next level by modeling what success looks like and perhaps most importantly, by helping you avoid the mistakes and common pitfalls that can derail your career.

Where to Find a Mentor or Coach

Mentors and coaches are everywhere! Here are some of the places you may find them:
- Your Industry.
- Your Company.
- Professional Associations.
- Trade Associations.
- Chambers of Commerce.
- Places of Worship.
- Colleges and Universities.

How to Approach a Mentor or Coach

The best way to approach a mentor or coach, especially if you're asking them to volunteer their time to meet with you, listen to you and give you advice that they acquired by paying their dues in the proverbial 'school of hard knocks', is to become aware of and honour the value of what you are asking for. The question you want to ask yourself is, "Why should this person help me?" And the answer to that question should have embedded in it the benefit to them for helping you; what is referred informally as WIIFM—What's in it for me—in this case, what's in it for them.

Again, you are positioning yourself as a partner in their cause, whatever that cause is, that is mutually beneficial to the both of you, and not just coming hat in hand for a favor or handout.

So here is how to approach and request the help, advice, and support of a mentor or coach. Learn as much about them as you can:

- Biography
- Publications
- Contributions to their field
- Causes and charities
- Anything else that can help you develop rapport

After you have gathered all the information you want, ask yourself "What can I do for them?" And you can do a lot. You can:

- Contribute to their cause or charity either by volunteering or offering to make a monetary donation.
- Make a connection for them if you know someone, or you are a member of a group they could benefit from.
- Offer a testimonial on how they helped you and the results you achieved with their help.
- Pay it forward by pledging to nurture and support others as you become more established in your career.
- Any other benefit you can bring...

Strategic Move #3 Develop the Entrepreneur's Mindset

When I was growing up I never entertained the thought of becoming an entrepreneur or going into business for myself. The path mapped out by my teachers in high school was to go to university and become a professional. I never associated practicing a profession with conducting a business, even though that's what professionals do in selling their services. I stumbled into business only after being laid off and going through the humiliation of being considered "unemployed" and the frustration of pounding the pavements looking for a job.

Business and entrepreneurial skills are crucial for survival in this brave new world of accelerated change where industrial society is giving way to a knowledge based economy. As this process unfolds, old industries die even as new ones begin to emerge. Accompanying this are massive shifts in the way economies distribute jobs, resulting in millions of people around the world losing high paying manufacturing jobs and having to retool and acquire new skills to survive.

There is no such thing as job security anymore. During the course of one's working life one can expect to have anywhere from three to five new careers. The worker of the future will have to commit him or herself to continuous learning and to be flexible and adaptable enough to change with the times.

The people who have survived and thrived in good, and especially in bad times, are entrepreneurs because of their ability to see and seize opportunity when others see problems. A survey of first generation millionaires in the United States found that the majority were entrepreneurs and business owners. Billionaire Bill Gates, the founder of Microsoft and Steve Jobs, a co-founder of Apple, are two notable examples.

The same holds true in Canada. Michael Lee Chin, an immigrant from Jamaica, and founder of AIC, a wealth management and mutual fund, which he later sold to Manulife Financial, is the first black Canadian billionaire. Another immigrant to Canada from Austria, who became a billionaire as a businessman and entrepreneur, is Frank Stronach. He founded Magna International in 1957, and nurtured it from its humble beginnings in his garage to become one of the largest auto parts manufacturing companies in the world.

Who is an Entrepreneur?

An entrepreneur is a special breed of person. The *Collins English Dictionary*, defines an entrepreneur, as, "the owner or manager of a business enterprise, who by risk and initiative, attempts to make profit." The emphasis here is on *risk* and *initiative*. Note also, the phrase "*attempts to make profit.*" There really is no guarantee of success and this is one of the defining characteristics of an entrepreneur—the capacity to tolerate huge doses of uncertainty. So let us take a look at the elements of the entrepreneur's mindset.

Elements of the Entrepreneur's Mindset

The elements of the Entrepreneur's Mindset are similar, or the same as the elements of the Achiever's Mindset which we discussed earlier, and the ways in which you develop the Entrepreneur's Mindset are also the same. It may be useful to review the elements of the Achiever's Mindset before going any further.

So here are the elements of the Entrepreneur's Mindset that pave the way for the entrepreneur's success.

1. **A clear vision of what they want to accomplish**. Successful entrepreneurs have a good sense of what they want to do, what they want to accomplish, with definite timelines. They have clearly written mission statements, short and long term goals which are derived from their mission statements that they consult on an ongoing basis to determine where they are in relation to their goals.
2. **High Self Confidence and Self Esteem**. Successful entrepreneurs feel good about themselves. They know that they are capable and worthy of achieving great things and don't allow critics in their circle to prevent them from pursuing their dreams.
3. **The ability to take risks and tolerate huge doses of uncertainty**. Successful entrepreneurs are calculated risk takers. Everyone who starts their own business undertakes huge personal and financial risks and although all entrepreneurs expect to be successful, there are no absolute guarantees that success will follow. The would-be entrepreneur needs to acknowledge the possibility of failure and still be one hundred percent committed to the success of his/her enterprise.
4. **The ability to manage stress well**. Stress becomes a close companion of entrepreneurs

who have to put in long hours and are constantly prospecting for new customers, contracts and projects to ensure a steady stream of revenue. Successful entrepreneurs are conscious of a balanced and healthy lifestyle and strive to take care of themselves.

5. **The ability to manage time well.** Successful entrepreneurs in the early stages of their enterprise wear several hats at the same time. They are the president, the delivery person, the janitor, the customer service representative, the sales person and much more. They are be able to prioritize and invest in those activities that will bring them the best returns on their investment of time.

6. **Openness to learn, to try something new and not to fear failure.** Successful entrepreneurs are creative thinkers and problem solvers, constantly seeking new, more efficient and effective ways of creating value for their customers and themselves. Most people refrain from trying something new because they fear failure more than they desire success. Successful entrepreneurs are driven more by the desire for success than their fear of failure.

7. **Optimistic.** Successful entrepreneurs have a positive "can do" attitude. They prefer to see the glass as being half full instead of it being half empty. This ability to reframe their perspective to emphasize the positive gives them the

resilience to bounce back from disappointing experiences.
8. **Disciplined**. Successful entrepreneurs have the ability to set goals, deadlines, and plans and to stick to them in spite of the temptation to engage in more pleasurable short term pursuits.
9. **Self-motivated**. Successful entrepreneurs are driven from within. They set their own challenges rather than allowing external peer and environmental pressures to dictate their actions.
10. **The ability to think creatively and create new opportunities where others see obstacles**. Successful entrepreneurs have the ability to bring new perspectives to old problems, to intuit new trends, tastes, and shifts in the market long before others who spend their time resisting change. The result is that they become trend setters and innovators, capitalizing on new opportunities even before others respond.
11. **The ability to build and sustain relationships**. Successful entrepreneurs have the ability to build and sustain relationships with customers, creditors, suppliers and others that they have to interact with on an ongoing basis. They genuinely like the people they work with and are themselves easy to get along with.
12. **Assume full responsibility for themselves**. Successful entrepreneurs don't blame others for their setbacks and misfortunes. They look first

at their own role to see what lessons they can learn and move on.

Successful entrepreneurs acquire the mindset, personal characteristics and technical skills they need to succeed by modeling other successful entrepreneurs; by seeking out coaches and mentors, even if they have to pay for it; and by reading extensively and committing themselves to a process of lifelong learning. Above all, they are committed to personal excellence and integrity in their personal and business affairs.

The challenges of becoming an entrepreneur are great but the risks are in proportion to the rewards. Becoming an entrepreneur opens you to the exciting possibility of becoming independently wealthy. Most of the millionaires in the world are business owners. A well-off owner operator of a small trucking company told me that he could not work for anyone because he could not stand the thought of having someone determine how much he could earn.

Even if you don't become an entrepreneur, the mindset along with branding and positioning yourself as President of 'You Inc.' and consultant to the company that employs you rather than just being an employee, will make you unstoppable as you launch your career. You will create value and opportunity for yourself and others throughout your working life. You will increase your odds of being seen as one of the MVPs (Most Valuable Players/Producers), in your company and hence more likely to survive and thrive even when there are downturns in the economy and decisions are made to let people go.

For clarity and brevity here are the comparisons between the Entrepreneur and Employee Mindset

Entrepreneur Mindset	*Employee Mindset*
Works to solve problems and create value.	Works to complete tasks and engages in busy work.
Focuses on and is rewarded for results.	Work equals pay, even if the work produces no tangible results.
Driving question, "How Can I Serve and Increase Value?" Concerned about "What keeps the boss awake at nights and what can I do to help?"	Driving Question, "What's In It For Me?" Not concerned with the boss's problems. That's why he gets the big bucks.

Skills of the Successful Entrepreneur

We've just covered the mindset, characteristics and behaviors of the successful entrepreneur. I want to talk now about some of the essential skills you will need in order to run your own business. I strongly believe that regardless of your major, everyone entering college or university should take some introductory elective courses in business. Here are the courses I would focus on:

- How to Lead and Manage People
- Marketing
- Sales
- Basic Business Accounting

There are also some basic skills in technology that will enhance your ability to communicate and scale your business that you should acquire. These are:

- How to create a compelling PowerPoint Presentation
- How to create a simple WordPress Website
- How to record and edit Video and Audio
- How to upload Audio and Video files to the internet

As a millennial who has grown up in the age of the internet, YouTube, Facebook and Twitter, these are skills that you already have or may have acquired as you played with your Apple and Android devices. The point I want to emphasize is that these are very important and useful skills that will serve you well if you decide to go into business for yourself.

What's more, these are skills that will serve you well in the workplace. Odds are only the most savvy boomers will have any proficiency in these skills. With these skills you can bring a lot of added value to your workplace and give you a competitive edge.

How to Choose a Business

You may now be wondering, "What type of business should I get involved in?" Earlier we discussed the importance of finding your mission and purpose and gave you a process to discover your passion, your values, your gifts and talents and the kind of career that would match those gifts and talents.

Those same considerations apply for the type of business you would get involved with. It should be one that you are passionate about and allows you to engage and express your gifts and talents. It should also be one where there are customers who are hungry for the goods or services you provide.

Network Marketing

Starting and running a business can cost a great deal of upfront investment in time and money. When I talk about starting and running a business I don't mean that you have to rent an office and employ staff. Ideally you should be able to start and run your business, at least the first one, out of your home with very little start up and carrying costs using your laptop and internet connection and without investing in lots of inventory.

A business model that allows the freedom and flexibility to do this is network marketing. There are many companies in many different niches, from health and wellness to financial services, who distribute their goods and services through network marketing. They cut out the retailer or middleman and go directly from the factory to the consumer using the power of the networks and associations, friends, family and neighbors to distribute their goods and services. The profit goes directly to the people in those networks.

David Bach, the wealth creation guru and author of *Start Late, Finish Rich* recommends getting involved with a network marketing company as a rapid way to build wealth. The advantages of getting involved with a network marketing company according to him are:

1. The company has a product or service and a tried and proven marketing system and tools.
2. Starting is relatively inexpensive.
3. You can gain access to coaching and training from people who are successful in that business and whose continued success is based on developing leaders such as yourself.
4. Your success is based on building and leveraging the collective efforts of the individuals you've sponsored into the organization.

Strategic Move #4 Master Your Money

Earlier, I talked about having a mission statement that included wealth as one of your goals. Wealth, according to the millionaires I've studied, have two dimensions to it. The first and most important dimension according to them is that wealth is an attitude, an orientation to the world.

They assert almost unanimously that if they were stripped of all their worldly possessions they would regain them in no time because they had mastered the inner game of wealth. One even noted that your wealth is what is left after you have lost all your money! The physical assets that we typically see as wealth—money, real estate, and investments are merely the manifestation of who they had become as individuals.

And to become that person who attracted wealth and abundance they had to overcome their limiting beliefs and build positive attitudes, supportive beliefs and the self-esteem and confidence to believe that they were worthy and capable of achieving wealth and financial freedom, using the affirmation and visualization tools I mentioned earlier.

Another psychological barrier people have to overcome are their limiting beliefs as they relate specifically to money itself. T. Harv Eker, author of the *Secrets of the Millionaire Mind* and creator of the *Millionaire Mind Intensive* Workshop, argues that the challenges and difficulties people have about money are directly related to their limiting beliefs about it. He maintains that we all have a money blueprint—an internal model of our financial success and unless we examine and debunk the limiting beliefs we have about money itself, then we will continue to sabotage ourselves.

Here are a few limiting beliefs about money I've come across:

1. To get rich I have to do something bad or dishonest.
2. If I get rich people won't like me for who I am but for my money.
3. I am not worthy enough or good enough to be rich.
4. Most of the good opportunities are gone.
5. The only ways I can be rich is to inherit it or to win the lottery.
6. Money is the root of all evil.

7. I don't know anything about money.
8. I am too young to get rich.
9. I am too old to get rich.
10. I am not educated enough to get rich.

So what are *your* limiting beliefs about money? After you have identified your limiting belief take each one and turn it into an affirmation. For example, the very popular limiting belief that money is the root of all evil could be turned around thus: "Money allows me to do a great deal of good in the world."

Your Money Acquisition Plan (MAP)

As effective as the tools I've shared are in removing the psychological barriers to acquiring wealth, you still need what I call a Money Acquisition Plan and to *take action* in fulfilling that plan. Here are some actions you should take:

1. Invest in your financial literacy. It is amazing how little we know about money—how to get it, keep it, grow it and pass it on as a legacy. There are many good books and courses you can take. Check out what gurus such as Warren Buffet are saying. You Tube is a starting point for information.
2. Find a certified financial planner who comes well recommended from someone you know whose portfolio has grown with the help of this person. Your financial planner must be more than just someone hired by a financial institution to sell you

financial products on a commission basis. You may also want to enquire about their own net worth.
3. Seek out someone you know who has accumulated wealth and ask them to mentor you.
4. Determine the amount of money you want to make and by when.
5. Write the amount down as an affirmation. E.g. I will have (x) amount by (date).
6. On your Vision Board include the pictures that represent your financial success--the house you want to live in, the car you want to drive, the places you want to travel to, the experiences you want to give yourself and your family.
7. Start saving and investing now.

Two Key Wealth Accumulation Principles

Ideally, everyone who has marketable skills and has spent 25 to 30 years employed in a job or career that pays them enough to take care of the bills and have some thrills should go into their retirement years with a certain amount of financial security. Yet the sad fact is that many face retirement saddled with debt and an old age circumscribed by lack. This condition could be avoided if at the beginning of their working life they put a plan in place for accumulating wealth. The problem is that most of us become consumers rather than investors, procrastinators rather than action takers.

Before we know it, we find ourselves facing a bleak future in what really should be our golden years. So what can those of us who have some time on our side do to ensure that our golden years are just that? Here are two key principles of wealth creation that we can follow:

1. **Pay yourself first.**
   This principle ingrains the habit of saving in us. Most of us pay everyone but ourselves first. The aim is to save 10% of your income and invest it so that the money works for you, instead of you working for it. The idea is to create multiple streams of passive income through your investment strategy.

This is where you work with a certified financial planner who will help you determine your financial goals, the level of risk you can tolerate, how much you should be putting away based on the number of working years you have before retirement.

2. **Budget.**
   Many people have no idea what is their income and expenditure. The cardinal rule is not to spend more than you earn. T. Harv Eker has designed a system which he argues is the easiest and most effective way to manage your money, and which allows you to save, invest and splurge, all at the same time.

He suggests that you separate your income into six different accounts, each for a specific purpose divided as follows:

1. **Necessity (NEC) Account**—50-55%. This account covers rent/mortgage; food, shelter, clothing. If your necessities take up more than 50-55% of your income, you need to either increase your income or cut back on expenditure in this category.

2. **Financial Freedom (FFA) Account**—10%. This is never spent and is used for investment. This is the account for your retirement income.

3. **Long Term Savings for Spending (LTSS) Account**—10%. This is for big ticket items such as a car. If you're in debt, then 5% of the money in this account goes toward debt servicing.

4. **Education (EDUC) Account**—10 %. This is as important as the FFA Account. You need to constantly upgrade your skills to stay current in a knowledge driven economy.

5. **Play Account**—10%. This account is for you to splurge on yourself! The one requirement is that you blow it on yourself in any way you choose. You are also to spend it monthly or quarterly.

6. **Give**—This varies between 5% and 10% depending on what you choose. People use this account as their tithing account.

The genius of T. Harv's system is that embedded in it are very sound wealth creation principles and in following this system you will end up building assets instead of accumulating liabilities. You can literally eat your cake and have it too!

The Magic of Compound Interest

Einstein is credited with saying that, *"compound interest is the eighth wonder of the world. He who understands it, earns it. He who doesn't, pays it."* What does he mean? Compound interest can work for you and it can work against you depending on whether you are saving and investing or consuming and putting yourself in debt.

So what is compound interest? According to Richard Croft and Eric Kirzner, co-authors of *The Beginner's Guide to Investing*, compound interest is interest that is paid on interest accumulated from prior periods. The example they offer is an investment of $1,000, earning 10% interest compounded annually. At the end of the first year your investment would have grown to $1,100 ($1000 x 1.10). This represents the original investment of $1,000 plus the interest earned on the principal.

If you reinvested the entire amount for another year, the investment would appreciate to $1,210. Here you would have earned $100 on the original investment plus $10 interest on the interest earned in the first year. If you were to leave this investment to compound over a period of 25 years, that $1000 would grow to $10,834.71.[2]

---

[2] You can find compound interest calculators by Googling the term.

In the two key wealth accumulation principles I spoke about earlier, I mentioned paying yourself first by saving and investing 10% of your income. I also mentioned T. Harv Eker's budgeting system in which he recommended opening a Financial Freedom Account (FFA) and saving 10% of your income which you would invest. Financial planners call this process of earmarking 10% of your income for investment the 10% principle. Now suppose that you committed yourself to saving 10% of your income and investing it over the course of your working life and you started working at age twenty five. That would put you in the workforce for forty years, if you retired at age sixty five.

Suppose also you average over the course of your working life only $30,000 per annum, which from any reasonable perspective would be ridiculous, because as you grow and develop in your career and increase the value you add to your employer, clients and customers your salary and income will increase. But I want to stay modest just to illustrate the magic of compounding.

So let's say on a monthly basis you put away 10% of your income ($250) at an annual average interest rate of 5%, which again is quite modest. How much would that be over the course of your working life of 40 years? You would have saved $120, 250.00. The interest accumulated on your savings would be $251,651.14 for a combined balance of $373,901.14. You would have essentially tripled your money over the period.

What that means if you had a money machine (which is what compound interest plus time really is), is that for every $1 you put in your machine you get back $3. That is a pretty good deal, which gets even better if you increase the amount you put in at higher rates of interest. Just by saving 10% of your income on a monthly basis over the course of your working life would virtually guarantee that your "golden years" are truly golden, especially when you combine that with other assets you probably would have accumulated.

Debt—The Obstacle in Your Wealth Accumulation Strategy

The major obstacle in your wealth accumulation strategy is debt. And you start accumulating debt when you take out your student loan. What is perhaps more insidious is credit card debt. From the first day on campus you are besieged by banks to take out a credit card. They tell you that it is important to establish a credit profile and the system is built to encourage that. The problem for most people is that the so-called credit profile all too easily becomes a *debt* profile, more so, if you fall into the habit of racking up credit card debt and paying back only the minimum payment each month. Credit card companies love when you carry a monthly balance. That's how they make their profits. They charge you compound interest on the debt. Compound interest, as I noted before, is a double edged sword. It works for you if you save and invest and it works against you if you accumulate debts.

To get a sense of how long it takes to pay off a credit card debt if you only pay the minimum, Google "debt interest calculator" and you will find free tools that will help you calculate how long it will take you to pay off a debt. Here is a hypothetical example. If you owe $1000 compounded annually at 23.9% and paying say $25 per month, it would take you over 82 months to pay the bill and you would incur interest charges of $1006.76.

Your debt will also impact your credit rating especially if you miss or skip payments. The more your credit rating dips, the more difficult it will be for you to get loans to start a business or pay down on a mortgage, so maintaining your creditworthiness is part of your own personal branding.

Assets vs. Liabilities

In his book *Rich Dad Poor Dad*, which I highly recommend, Robert Kiyosaki talks about the importance of distinguishing between assets and liabilities. Assets put money in your pocket and increase your wealth; liabilities take money out of your pocket and decrease your wealth. The following table gives you a comparison of Assets vs. Liabilities:

Assets	*Liabilities*
Cash	Debt
Stocks	➢ Credit Card
Bonds	➢ Consumer Loans
Mutual Funds	Taxes
Real Estate	Mortgages
Precious Metals	

The aim is to increase your assets and have your assets become what my mentors refer to as 'multiple streams of income' while at the same time minimizing your liabilities. If you take on debt the intention must be to use it as short term leverage to increase your assets.

What I've shared with you here is only intended to whet your appetite and give you some broad and general principles about wealth and wealth creation. Given the volatility in the world economic system and the trend that over your lifetime you will have to stitch together several different careers to have the 20 or 30 year career your parents had, you should expect that there may be periods of unemployment and reduced opportunities for saving and investing. It is therefore most important for you to know how to manage your money and find ways to generate your income from your assets.

Summary

In this chapter I outlined the four practical and strategic moves you need to make to ensure that you successfully launch your career and accumulate enough wealth over time to guarantee that your golden years are truly golden. The four moves are:

1. Market and Position Yourself
2. Find a Mentor or Coach
3. Develop the Entrepreneur's Mindset
4. Master Your Money

Each of these moves was further broken down to give you a step by step process of executing them. Here are some of the highlights. In move number one, marketing and positioning yourself in the job market, you need to determine the value you bring to potential employers and clients and communicate that effectively to them. Two essential communication skills are public speaking and managing interpersonal conflicts. Both will give you a competitive advantage.

In move number two, finding and approaching a mentor, you need to find out all you can about this person, determine what's in it for them to mentor you and make it worth their while. A good way to do so is to contribute to a cause that is dear to them either by volunteering your services or making a monetary donation.

In move number three, you need to develop the entrepreneurial mindset and take this approach to your career. You also need to develop some entrepreneurial skills. Two key skills are marketing and sales. If you choose to start a business, you should choose a field that you're passionate and knowledgeable about, and for which there is a market willing to pay for the goods or services you offer.

Finally, in move number four, I talked about mastering your money so that you will become financially free, liberating yourself from the necessity of a job and generating your income from the assets you accumulate. Some highlights in this area include becoming financially literate, letting go of your limiting beliefs about money, budgeting, paying yourself first and minimizing debt while increasing your assets.

Conclusion

If you have read up to this point you now know the three mission critical strategies you need to launch a successful career and live an awesome live. What's more, you have been given the tips, tools and techniques you need to put these strategies into play in your own life. The three Strategies can be summed up succinctly as Mission, Mindset and Moves as follows:

1. Clarify your *Mission* and Purpose.
2. Cultivate the Achiever's *Mindset*.
3. Execute the strategic *Moves* to achieve your dreams.

You are now in a much better position than I was when I embarked on my career. The wisdom and knowledge I've shared with you have cost me a great deal in time, energy and money to acquire. This is my gift to you. It will save you a great deal in time, energy, money and frustration and give you a competitive advantage in the marketplace if you implement what you've learned.

The key here is to take action. Having knowledge without taking action is the equivalent of not having the knowledge in the first place. If you need support and further coaching to implement the strategies I've outlined, you can contact me at LarryJohanson2@gmail.com to explore how I can further support you.

You are part of a generation that will soon come in to its own and assume control over the running of your society and the world. The future is bright and the opportunities are endless but the challenges are also great. My hope is that what I've shared with you here will help you create a life for yourself—of health, wealth, wisdom and happiness—and that these principles will be the cornerstone of your contribution to the world.

Best of luck!

Courses, Seminars, Workshops

Becoming Leaders

Becoming Leaders is a general introductory course for individuals who are interested in becoming leaders to explore what it means to be a leader, and define the skills and traits required to become inspiring and effective leaders. Through a simulation game, participants get an opportunity to experience the impact of different leadership styles on the teams they lead and to integrate experientially the concepts discussed.

Effective Presentation Skills

This two day workshop is a practical, 'hands on' experience of preparing and presenting an effective presentation. Participants are asked to come with a formal presentation that they are required to give. The presentations are videotaped and combined with observations from other participants, become part of a thorough and constructive feedback process.

Participants are required to incorporate the feedback into a new presentation and have an opportunity to compare the new presentation and delivery with the previous one. The facilitator complements this process with a presentation on how to prepare and give effective presentations. Class sizes are limited to 10 because of the intense one on one coaching involved in this workshop.

Managing Conflict

Although it is acknowledged that conflict can be a stressful and difficult experience for most individuals, participants in this seminar are encouraged to reframe conflict as an opportunity for constructive dialogue and resolution of differences. Individuals are asked to create a plan for resolving a current conflict using a range of time-honored prescriptions. A key focus is on managing one's own anger in the heat of the moment.

Mastering Breath Awareness

This workshop draws upon Larry's extensive experience of Zen meditation practice and is based on the perspective that the breath is the most effective natural tool to manage stress and create space for insight and growth. Participants gain an appreciation for the importance of breath awareness to their physical and mental health and are introduced to practices and exercises that can easily be integrated into their everyday lives.

www.ingramcontent.com/pod-product-compliance
Lightning Source LLC
Chambersburg PA
CBHW071147090426
42736CB00012B/2261